I0435469

Mini Guide
Essential Bathroom Planning

Brian Rider

Mini Guides 2016

Foreword

Thank you for choosing one of our New Mini Guides. The purpose of these guides is to provide a simple paperback training guide in a variety of KBB and Interior Designer or even Exterior Designer titles which extract the highly focussed information from our giant tomes that ran about 1000 pages and which would cost a lot more than you would wish to pay or we would wish to charge, With our mini guides you can acquire any of the titles at an extremely modes targeted sum.

1

COPYRIGHT

2

Essential Bathroom Planning

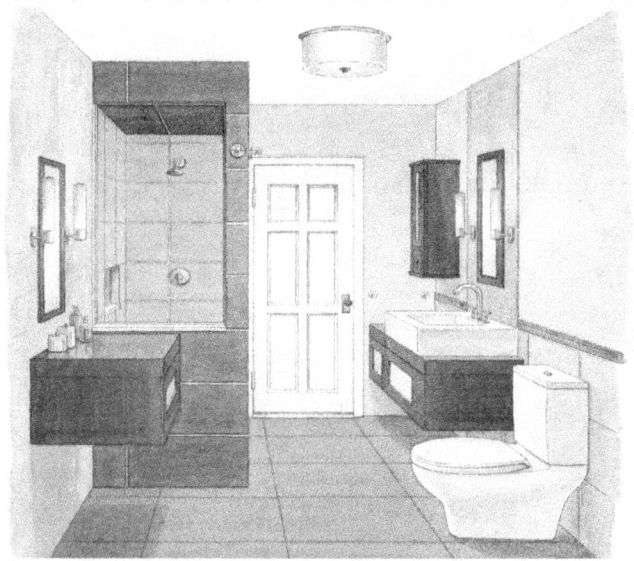

Bathroom planning is generally misunderstood even by installers and so called professional "designers". Indeed very few bathroom planners are capable of designing bathrooms and many bathroom "deigns" are extremely poor. In our professional **KBB** associations we awarded diploma for various levels of achievement. One was for **PLANNING** and a separate diploma for **BATHROOM DESIGN**. Of the 1000's of trainees through our courses most of them reach the **PLANNING** level but very, very few reached the **DESIGNER** level. It is important to do the basics well and then progress.

WHAT DO I NEED TO KNOW AS A BATHROOM PLANNER?

The products

If you don't know your product you are wasting you time

Plumbing

Absolutely essential for basic bathroom planning.

Basic planning guidelines & notation

If you cannot plan the essentials it will not work and will not be saleable

Rules and regulations

there are many rules established for a number of years and all covered by our planning rules sections. Failure to adhere to these rules may mean insurance companies will not reimburse in cases of accidents, even fire,

Services

If you don't know the essentials of services how can you plan?

Understanding Installation

You have to know what the limitations of the installer is and what equipment is available, No point in planning wall hung items if the installer cannot handle them.

WHAT DO I NEED TO KNOW AS A BATHROOM DESIGNER

all the foregoing plus an in depth knowledge of

Ergonomics and Anthropometrics

Ventilation

Macerators

Islands and Peninsula

Disable bathrooms

30° and 45ª solutions

Presentation Techniques

Personal vs Saleable

Fitted furniture bathrooms

Bathroom Storage

Section 1
BATHROOM Planning

REMEMBER

1. First do no harm
2. Make sure you understand the survey
3. Ensure you are familiar with planning presentation.
4. Ensure your plans are efficient and safe
5. Ensure you understand the customers needs & desires

You will need to study all the sections in the book and above all you will need to practice practice practice. We have provided exercises for you to complete on your journey to becoming a bathroom planner. You may aspire to become a bathroom designer but this is, in reality, a goal that few ever really achieve.

What is the definition of a BATHROOM PLANNER?

"someone who understands the product he/she is using and can place the sanitaryware accurately and efficiently.

Someone who can visit the project home and assess all the physical and service requirements and, where necessary,make efficient and productive alterations.

Someone who understands the sanitaryware requirements of and his/her portfolio of appliances and can make real and valid recommendations to the customer.

Someone who can liaise with the installer and who understands the abllities of the installer or simply produces a plan that is within the comprehension of any competent installer."

What is the definition of a BATHROOM DESIGNER?

" a bathroom designer must be able to offer all the skills of a bathroom planner and has practices those skills over a reasonable period of time and has executed good working projects.

A designer should be able to take a project to a higher level and provide inspired execution of the project incorporating design elements that will genuinely enhance both the look and the feel of the project.

A designer must be able to convey understanding of the design elements to both the customer and the installer. It is difficult to produce a design that can be easily executed without an understanding of the installer's capabilities."

PLANNED OK   NOW WITH DESIGN ELEMENTS

What are design concepts?

Design concepts are not just innovative sanitaryware. Indeed these are not really design in the true sense. Although they may be part of overall design they are not a basis for bathroom design.

Bathroom design should be producing a layout that not only has visual effect but has much enhanced features to make the project more versatile and useful.

For example incorporating a bath and a shower in the same room would be a huge benefit for most households.

An innovative furniture design might allow even a diy bathroom installer to use much higher quality products without the need for on site, expensive tooling.

To fully qualify as a DESIGNER BATHROOM the layout should incorporate advanced features that FIT THE BUDGET.

Finally, remember that installers often have never had proper training except possibly with regards to services so it is the Designer's function to ensure the fitter fully appreciates the function and execution of the design concepts and can assist on-site in their successful incorporation into the project. If you are not confident you can influence the installer it is probably best not to use any really advanced elements.

Type to enter text

3

The Measure - Survey

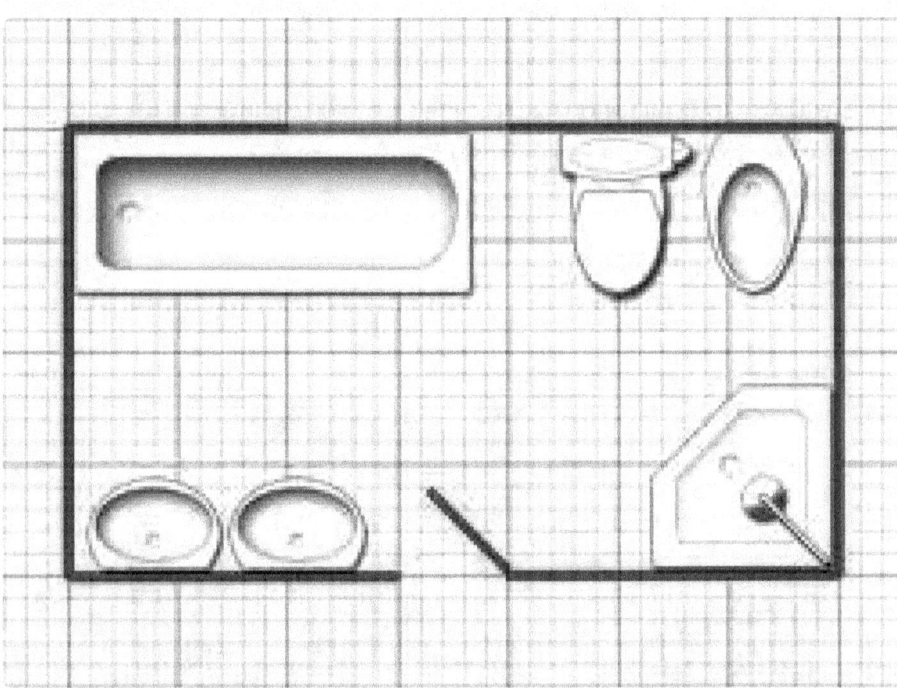

Before you can plan a bathroom you need to know the layout and measurements of the room and all the architectural features of the room. You also need to know the location of the services and you need to understand the limitations of altering these services

The Equipment you need

There are many different tools for measuring but the electronic are the best.

Laser Measuring Device

This is a typical laser measuring device accurate to within 1.5cm and can measure up to 40 metres. This one costs under £100 which is not a lot considering the speed and accuracy of the device. You should also back this up with another method - always measure with at least 2 devices.

There are also some other measuring deices which are probably now a little superfluous such as the ultrasonic and the infra red devices. These did not have the accuracy and are prone to mishandling and errors. It is now time to dispose of these outdated items When using a traditional tape for measuring you need to remember that they have a floating end which can be used to hook around something or compress to measure directly from the face of an object or part of the room. For normal measures there is no reason for this kind of accuracy as you should build in flexibility into your plan. Even if your measurements are accurate the room is probably not square and this will throw out your plan by as much as 40-50 mm at some point.

GOLDEN RULE

Always build in flexibility. There is one area where you need to be utterly accurate and that is with expensive counter tops. In most cases they cannot be easily worked on site and they are difficult to prepare and to cut so get it right the first time. In general terms the man made solid state surfaces can be worked afterwards to some degree - perhaps 2-3 cm. but some of the traditional solid surface materials such as marble and Granite or even slate do not have any realistic flexibility. If you are fabricating exotic countertops you want them to fit - first time.

One of the most common errors in measurements is not providing the correct spaces for Sanitaryware. BTW toilets provide the dimensions for the product but not the concealed cistern and Wall Hung toilets also will be best to install with special mounting frames. Maybe just for ventilation.

Showers are a big problem area because there are so many different shapes and sizes plus there is access and use space to consider. The shower tray will also require special consideration as there are many types of trays and many types of shower traps.

You will also need to understand the water supply and its limitations. No point in planning for a giant German shower head requiring 40litres a minute when you only have an electric shower?

Clearly if you are in the customer's home you don't want to spend hours on the initial measure.. If you are also trying to provide a plan on the night and possibly even sell on the night. timing is a critical consideration. Unless you are in an OTN environment it is usually best to do the most efficient measure possible and then produce your plan in the studio where you can ponder over any of the problems that might pop up.

This also gives you a chance to double check any queries you may have. Invite the buyer into the showroom to view the plan and the estimate. Always build in a few optional extra. Everyone has a budget no matter what they say. If you have a desirable extra, show them the cost and sell them the advantages. This way you should be able to come out with the sale even if it is just a basic deal.

Surprisingly bathrooms require a great deal more technical considerations than kitchens. The water has to come to the product and go away. I have planned many, many bathrooms where the previous installation just wasn't good enough. Typical problems are waste plumbing and ventilation. If you don't provide the correct ventilation the room will deteriorate quickly

A selection of measuring items.

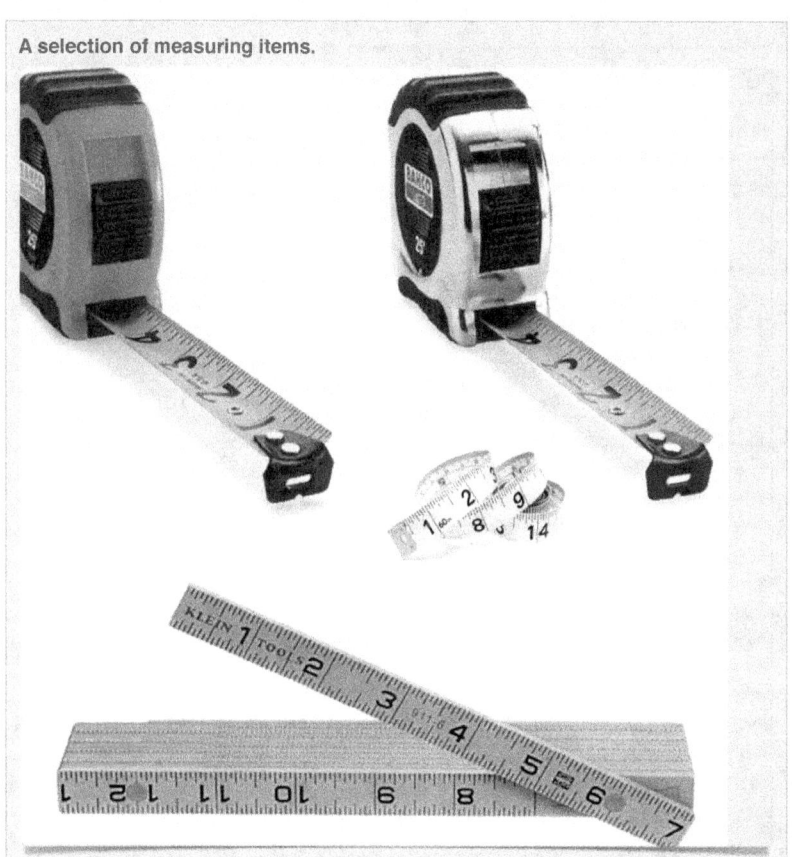

A steel tape is good for larger measures but the folding rule is the most versatile of all the items - up to 5 metres

Floor Plans

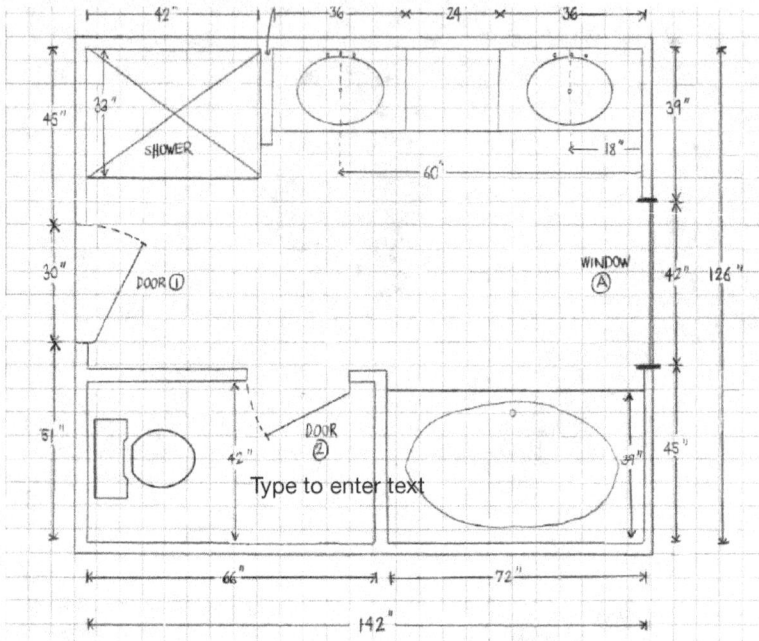

The floor plan is the vital first stage of Bath;room Planning. Firstly you need a working plan of the kitchen and services layout. It is vital to note all the key service positions plus the access to the main electrics, water and drainage.

The more accurate the floor plan the more accurate your kitchen plan and, in particular, the more practical that proposal will be.

Too many bathroom planners and designers try to place facilities where they are simply impractical. For example if you wanted to plan a bathroom with an island plumbing setting to incorporate sanitaryware how are you going to get the plumbing to it and more important how are you going to get the waste away. I have seen too many so called clever designers plan a bathroom in this way only to have to use a small bore pumping system to get the water away. The installation costs would be astronomical and the on going servicing problems would give the householder many problems.

Macerators are excellent for their purpose but in a main bathroom would you really want to put up with that noise all the time? As you start on your first bathroom planning efforts you will be best to keep it simple and don't move things about too much especially with the w.c. and it's large bore waste pipe.

Clearly an A4 drawing board would be a great help in these instances. Also remember to take along a basic drawing kit and scale rule and at least a red pen or perhaps a multicolour pen. It is amazing what you can forget unless it is clearly indicated and written down at the time. ACCURACY IS THE KEY. It is also highly recommended that you prepare a quick floor plan for the new kitchen to try out the ideas and get some feedback from the customer.   Even if you are working with a computer a manually drawn plan takes minutes and is a great help in producing your computer graphics. It also has the big benefit of demonstrating to the customer how professional you are.

A grasp of all the skills necessary for the completion of such an expensive project is part of the secret of selling the project.

Confidence is a big sales boost

Have a look at some of the floor plan examples we have shown here. Some very simple some quite elaborate.

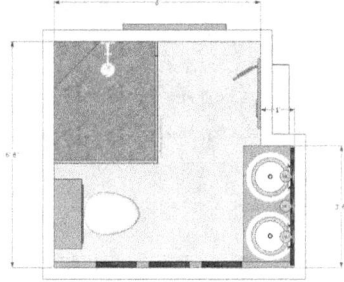

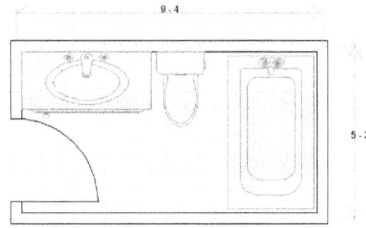

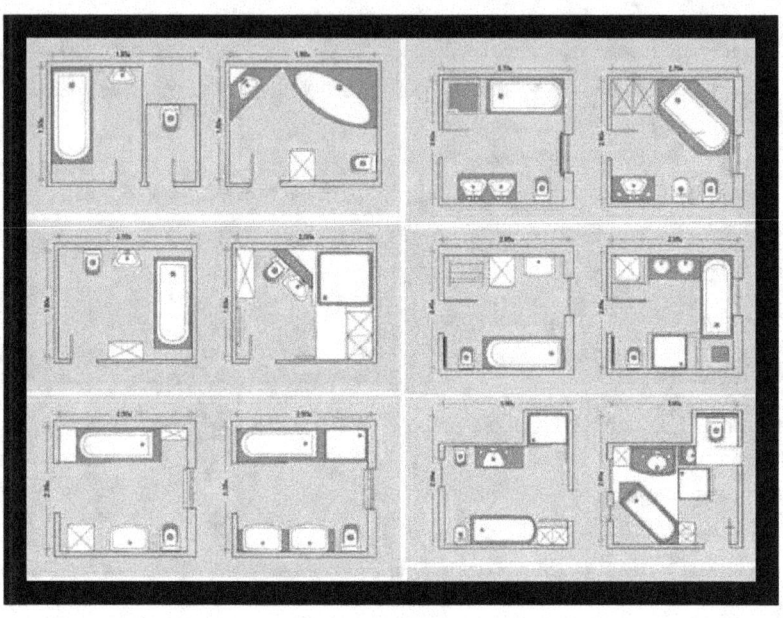

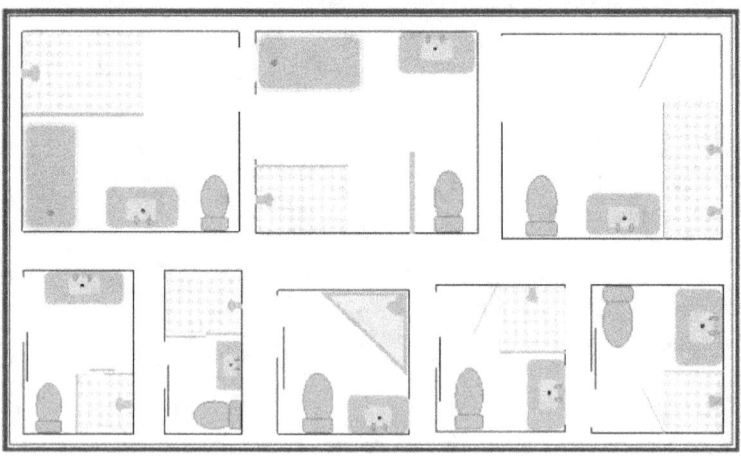

An axonometric survey plan is invaluable

If you want to learn this quick, simple drawing method we have a mini guide for this topic.

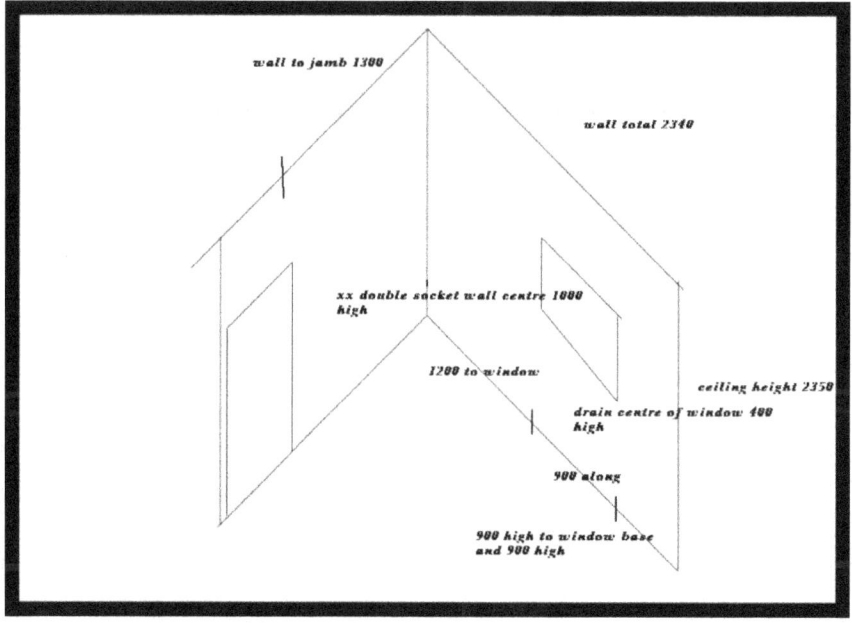

4

Clear Planning

There is no point in providing a plan unless it can be read by everyone.

Incorporating an elevation or a 3d presentation with your bathroom plan can be a great asset.

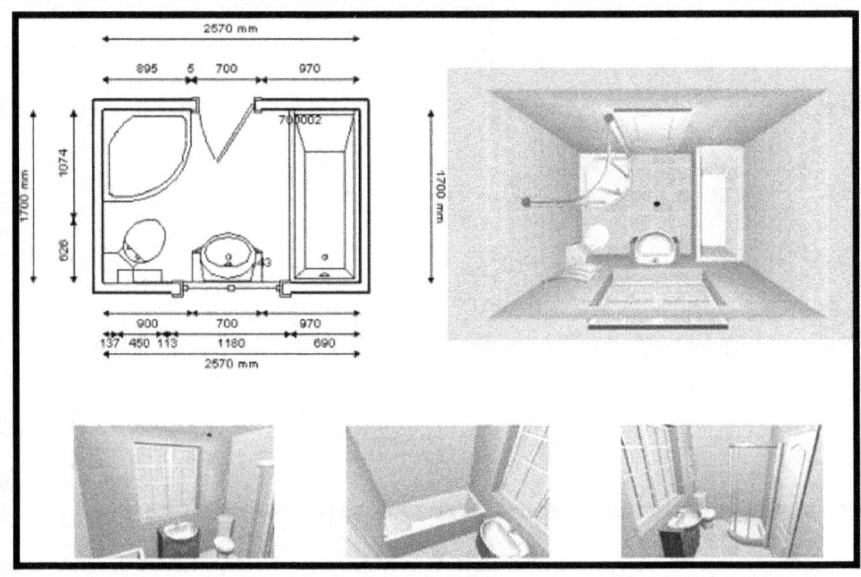

Drawing techniques & equipment

•always draw with the board or square, never freehand

•draw in pencil, a mechanical proper pencil is best

•the parallel should be locked to draw

•use a 45° and 60/30° for all angles

•use a light touch so the drawing can be altered

•use a copier to add further detail and keep a master

•always draw by hand and then transfer to a computer if you are using one

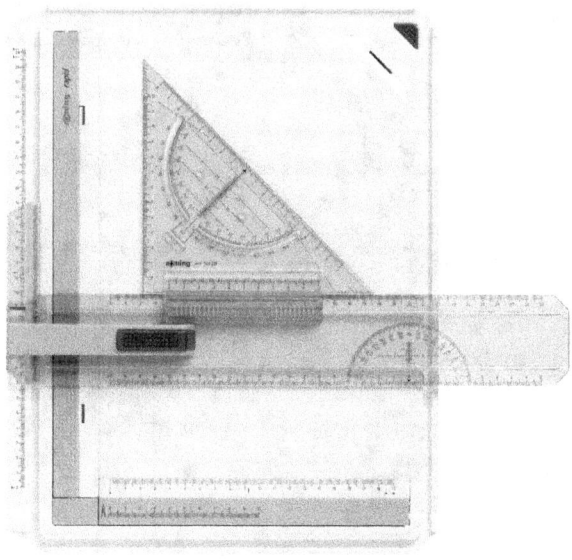

5

Planning

What are the planning rules regarding ergonomics and anthropometrics. What are the planning rules regarding services and sanitaryware. Are there any really rigid considerations that are peculiar to this area? Any restrictions as to service changes?

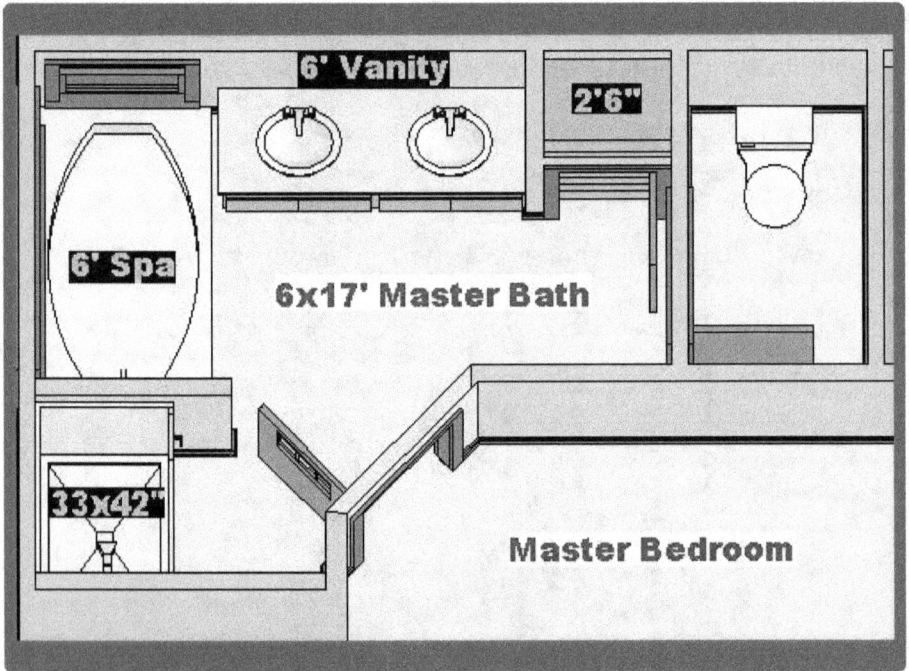

On the following pages we have listed the many rules that govern bathroom planning. Don't think you can ignore them as most of them are simply common sense. Many are also safety regulations usually enforced by ROSPA and always referred to be the insurance companies. Ignore a rule and cause injury or damage you an be in serious trouble.

Bathroom Planning Considerations

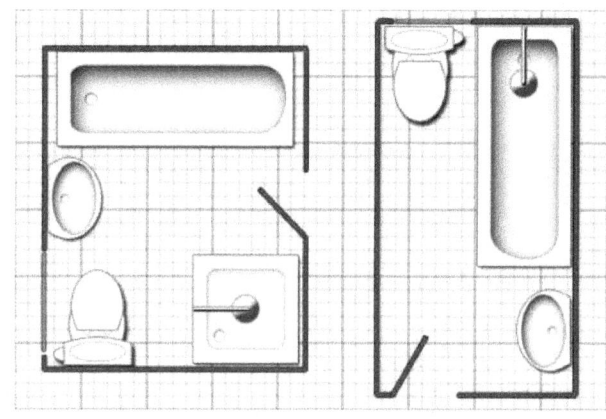

When you consider these two bathrooms there is something quite obvious. The **RH** room is poky but adequate. The **LH** room is only very slightly larger but a vast improvement and could even be more intelligently planned using more modern showers such as a quadrant.

Quite often you can find extra space just by incorporating an airing cupboard into the main bathroom or perhaps combining a separate w.c. into the main room.

After all it is hardly hygienic having a w.c. in a room where there is no hand washing facility.

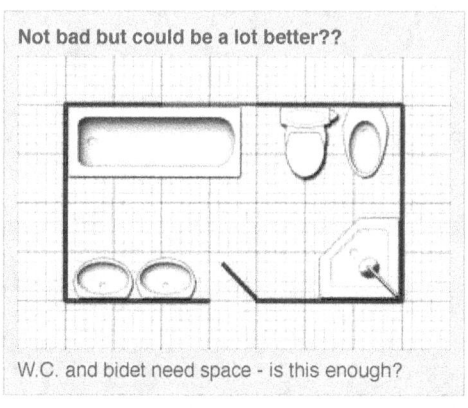

Not bad but could be a lot better??

W.C. and bidet need space - is this enough?

Planning Considerations

• What sanitaryware does the customer want?

• What sort of washbasin is required?

• What is the best layout for the room?

• What are the service limitations?

• Is a separate shower required?

• Is there a budget?

• Are there any items to be used?

• Are any items required later?

• What sort of style is required?

• Can I duct the extractor fan to atmosphere? Absolutely vital in a bathroom.

Clear Planning

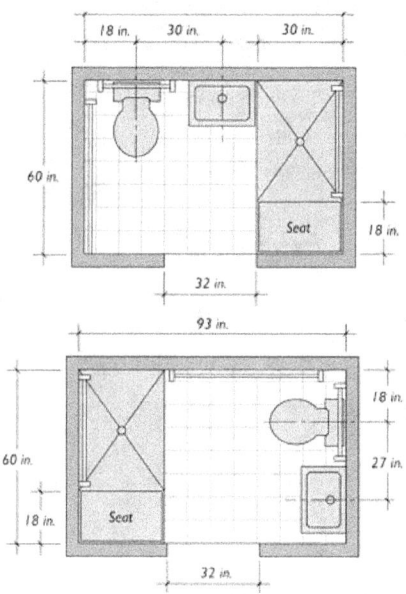

These two plans were presented by two different bathroom planners and they are both superficially efficient at least in terms of space. But where is the w.c. waste? Are we able to move it to these different positions? Measurements?

There is a small square to the left of the wc in the top plan, but this could easily be due to the graph paper and other lines so we cannot be sure.

In older houses in the U.K. they used a lot of S traps. i.e. the big waste pipe is under the floor and then goes to the inside or outside stack. However this is more likely to be on the window wall so neither plan would have addressed this problem. Clearly we need to know where this waste is and one plan must be unworkable. You can move most things in the bathroom but beware of the wc - this has a 100mm waste.

Planning for a Shower

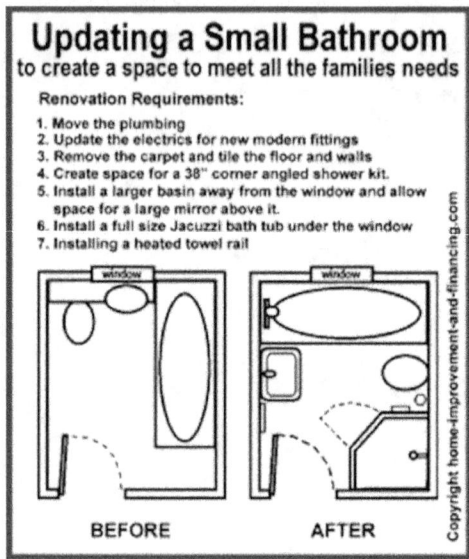

Updating a Small Bathroom
to create a space to meet all the families needs

Renovation Requirements:

1. Move the plumbing
2. Update the electrics for new modern fittings
3. Remove the carpet and tile the floor and walls
4. Create space for a 38" corner angled shower kit.
5. Install a larger basin away from the window and allow space for a large mirror above it.
6. Install a full size Jacuzzi bath tub under the window
7. Installing a heated towel rail

BEFORE   AFTER

Copyright home-improvement-and-financing.com

Superficially the plan seems to work but W.C.? The plan appears to show a btw or wall hung wc but where is the cistern. It should be shown on an efficient plan but not shown on this one. If they are trying to show a typical U.S. 1 piece wc it is not correctly drawn.

I always used to look at the possibilities of incorporating a shower in the bathroom. If this project was an ensuite then a shower would be the norm but if this was a smaller property with only one main master bathroom it is always wise to leave a bath and add a shower if possible. Property is not easily saleable in any sort of property without a bath. Many buyers will still prefer a bath. Although a huge percentage of people have opted to have showers in place of the bath there are still those who like the spa effect of luxuriating in a warm badedas bath.

However it must be said that I would always question the notion that you want to lie in your own filth.

People space is essential to allow working .movement and access in a bathroom.

This is quite an interesting conversion and uses some very high quality products. We have to assume that the owner is around 7 foot tall so he can reach the shelving over the shower. Equally he and she are clearly quite slim as there is less than 600mm to the left of the wc.

However the w.c. and combined sink is worth noting as if you have a customer who wants to keep his separate w.c. you can at least offer a product that allows hand washing in the room without going next door and plastering the door knob with germs. This idea was first used in Scandinavia and it works very well.

Always leave a logical amount of space for working and manoeuvring.

MICRO BATHROOM

This was clearly a cloakroom and has been adapted. There really isn't much space for the wetroom shower. The sink on top of the w.c. looks rather odd but it does work.

Ergonomics & Anthropometrics

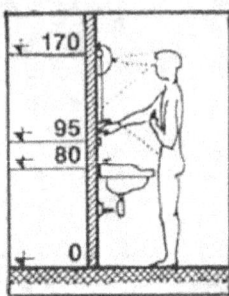 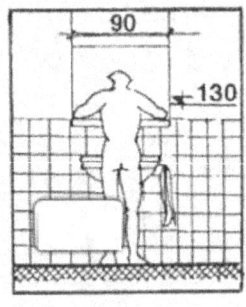 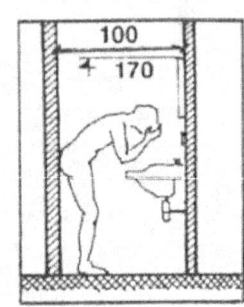

Space required for washing face (in cm)

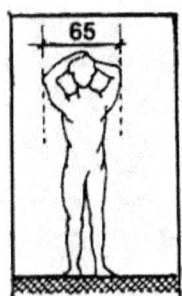 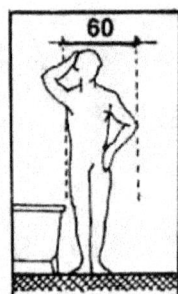 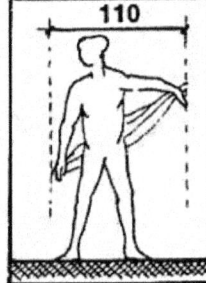 

Space required for using a towel (in cm)

A well planned Bathroom takes into account the ergonomic & anthropometric considerations of modern planning but tempered to a reasonable extent to the customer's needs.

Remember however, the more personal the bathroom the less saleable to a 3rd party.

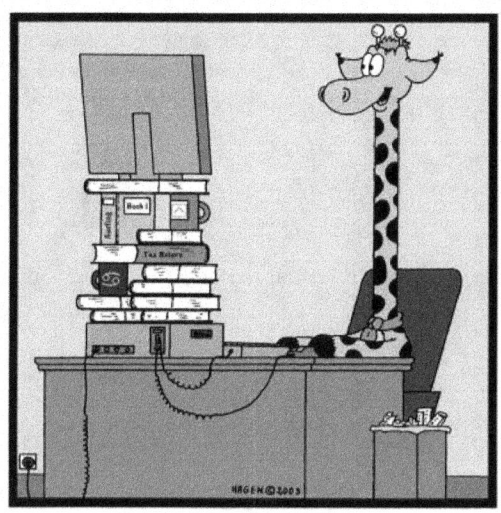

Now, that's more ergonomic...

Perhaps these illustration can suggest to the planner that it is important to take into account the physical attributes of the end user.

What is the definition of ERGONOMICS

"the study of people's efficiency in their working environment."

Definition of Anthropometry

A. "anthropometry, especially as it relates to the design of furniture and machinery."

B. The study of the human body and its movement.

**ANTHROPOMETRICS APPLIED
TO AN HAIR DRYER**

Anthropometric data (measurements) are used to determine
the shape of handle and distance to be held from head.
Designed for average size hand. The length of lead is
determined from anthropometric data (length of average
arms and average height of users). The hair dryer is now
ergonomically designed.

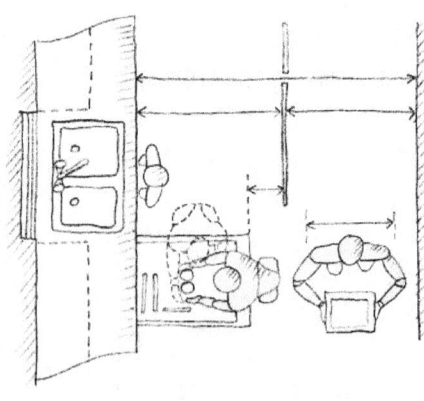

The link between anthropometrics and ergonomics

Anthropometrics is the comparative study of human body measurements and properties.

Ergonomics is the science of making the work & home environment safer and more comfortable for people using design and anthropometric data.

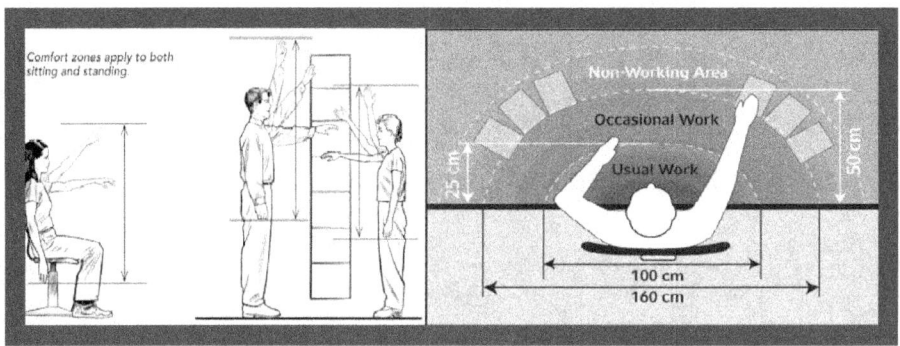

Comfort zones apply to both sitting and standing.

Non-Working Area

Occasional Work

Usual Work

25 cm

50 cm

100 cm

160 cm

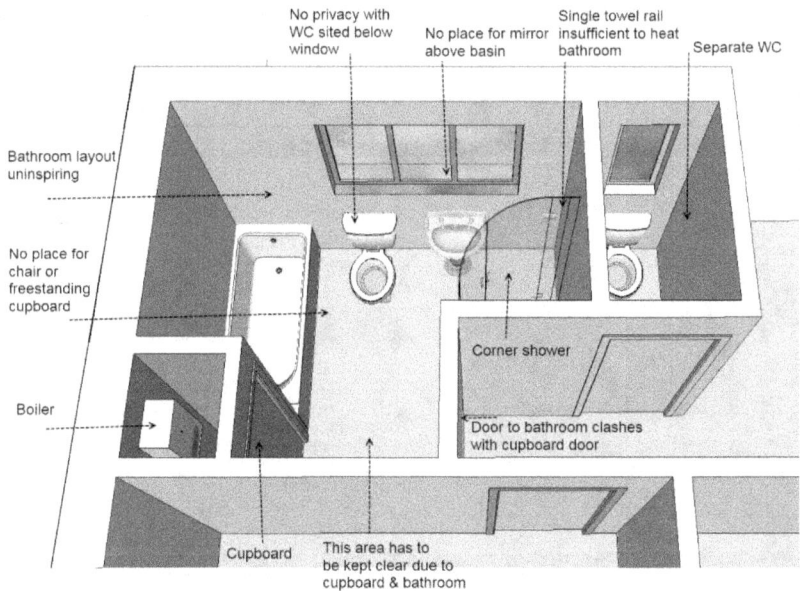

No privacy with WC sited below window

No place for mirror above basin

Single towel rail insufficient to heat bathroom

Separate WC

Bathroom layout uninspiring

No place for chair or freestanding cupboard

Boiler

Corner shower

Door to bathroom clashes with cupboard door

Cupboard

This area has to be kept clear due to cupboard & bathroom doors

ORIGINAL BATHROOM

Bathroom Layouts

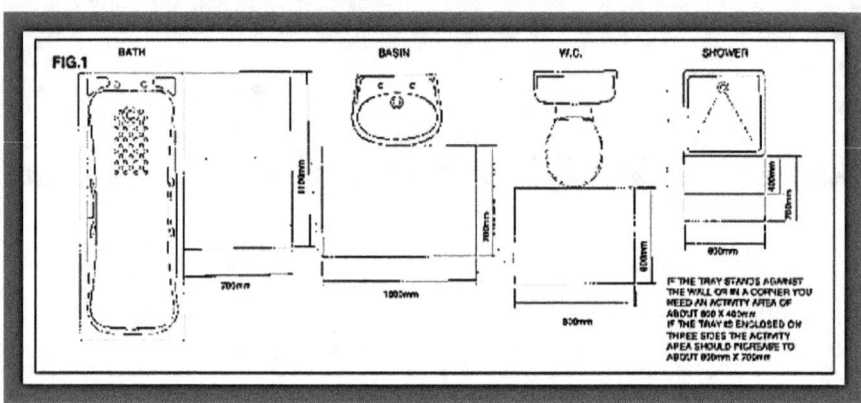

FIG.1 BATH   BASIN   W.C.   SHOWER

IF THE TRAY STANDS AGAINST
THE WALL OR IN A CORNER YOU
NEED AN ACTIVITY AREA OF
ABOUT 800 X 480mm
IF THE TRAY IS ENCLOSED ON
THREE SIDES THE ACTIVITY
AREA SHOULD INCREASE TO
ABOUT 800mm X 700mm

Most Bathrooms fall into a pattern of layouts similar to those shown here. All layouts must follow the safety and planning rules. Compact bathrooms will almost benefit from the modern compact sanitaryware especially w.c.'s with 6 litre flush or less.

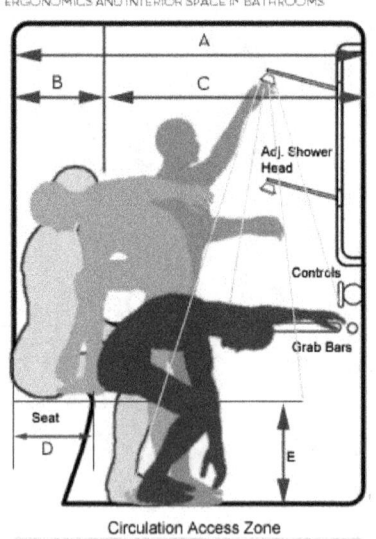

ERGONOMICS AND INTERIOR SPACE IN BATHROOMS

Adj. Shower Head

Controls

Grab Bars

Seat

Circulation Access Zone

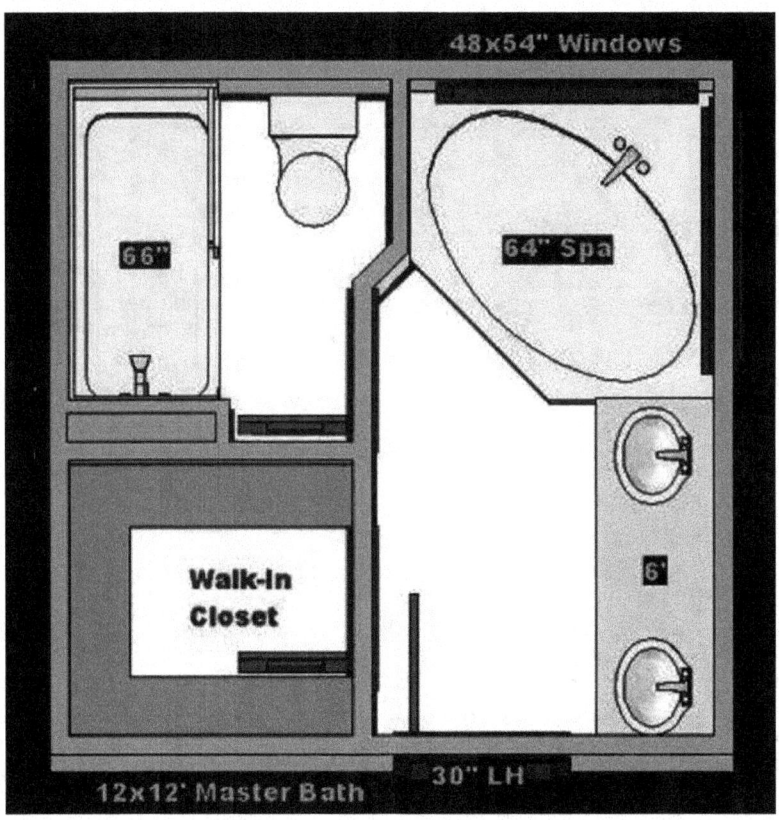

It is quite an attractive plan but the planner has forgotten the doors. The only indication of a door is to the bathroom proper. We will assume that as this is an American plan, (where the current and longstanding fetish is for a separate toilet) that there is a door between the main bathroom and the toilet which also seems to house a second bath?

Apart from that it seems to be quite an efficient plan but surely opening the room completely would have been a far better idea. We can assume where the outside walls are but it is not easy as the walls have not been shown correctly. Inside walls should be shown around 100mm and outside around 200mm or even 300mm. Why on earth would you want 2 baths? See end of book?

8

Sanitaryware & Fitments

Not everyone will have the same portfolio so you have to become fully conversant with all the products in your range and learn to plan efficiently and eventually, imaginatively with your products. For the time being, an innovative plan will capture the imagination of the customer against a boring but expensive plan.

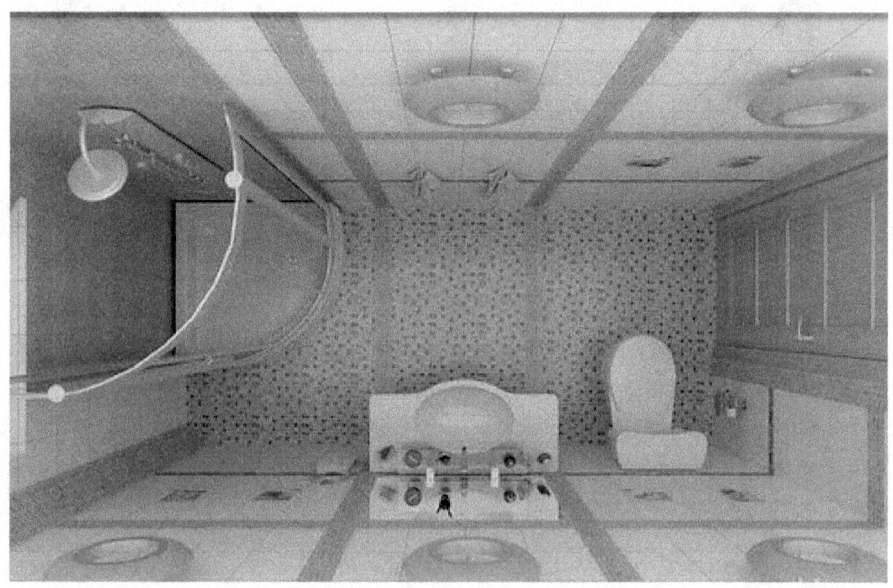

Baths

Clawfoot and pedestal baths (also called roll top baths)

- Recessed or alcove baths

- Inset baths

- Free standing baths

- Corner baths

- Whirlpool baths or Jacuzzis

- Walk-in or gated baths for disabled users

Baths are made in a whole variety of substances and finishes & colours. Many baths are designer items so we will not consider these as the buyer decides the budget. If can afford a designer bath you don't need to query the choice as you will be able to afford a replacement when you tire of it or when it starts to look shabby. Even a £5k bath could look shabby very quickly & the cheap Chinese spa baths costing £1-2K might only survive a year or two.

It pays to think very carefully about your choice. if you want a roll top bath always go for a double skinned genuine acrylic bath. The surface on these quarry stone type baths can be very difficult to maintain. Solid surface is wonderful for worktops but not so great for baths and can be quite limited strength wise.

NON-STANDARD BATHS

Alto double ended *Ideal Standard*   1700 x 750

Loussanne   1700 x 800
D535

Strasbourgh
Offset corner
1500 x 1000

Rennes   1700 x 850
D510

Metz   1685 x 850

Axis ⟲carron   1700 x 700
Easy access   D430

Spacemaker *Ideal Standard*   1700 x 700/550

Spacesaver VitrA   1700 x 750/500

Carla Eco Roca   1700 x 700
Easy access   D415

Washbasin

The type of basin will be dictated by the style of the bathroom. Basin sizes tend to be more restrictive with traditional style bathrooms so this may be a limiting factor.. Some of the traditional circular pedestals can be difficult to install and will probably need a flow through trap.. Pop up wastes are popular but rarely adjusted or installed properly. Remember your taps may be one tap hole - two tap hole - or three tap hole. Very few basins are available as 3 tap hole but it is possible to have them drilled - by a monumental mason (at your own risk). Many basins are semi punched so you can select your options at the site. Please note that few plumbers are capable. It is a quite easy task but you need a centre punch, a ball pane hammer and a steady nerve and eye. Cloak basins can be as small as 200mm.

W.C. SUITE

❖ *there is virtually no S trap just a pan connector*

❖ *you cannot legally install other than a 6/3 litre flush wc.*

❖ *almost all w.c. are now push button flush*

❖ *replacement cisterns are now a problem*

w.c.'s are more or less standard but not all dimensions are identical

The style of suite chosen by the customer will normally dictate the actual w.c. you will be working with. Most modern w.c. are quite compact and therefore quite easy to work with. Moving the w.c. from it's existing position is not that easy. In first floor bathrooms you will nearly always be working with the SVP which is usually in the corner of the room and you can clearly see how the w.c. is positioned in relation to the svp. Moving the w.c. closer to the svp is quite straightforward. Moving away from the svp along the same wall is also quite easy or possibly the adjacent wall. As a general rule you are best to keep the w.c. as short as possible to the stack but moving to the adjacent wall should not be a problem.

The quality of the w.c. should be an issue but rarely are they chosen for this reason. Generally speaking you will need to look at the German ranges to get some hi tech non stick finishes - very desirable.

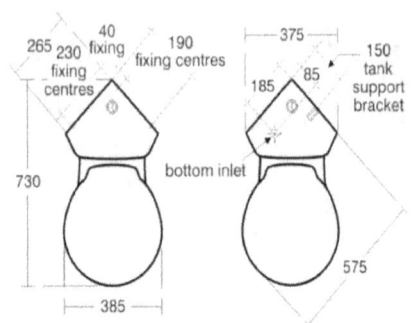

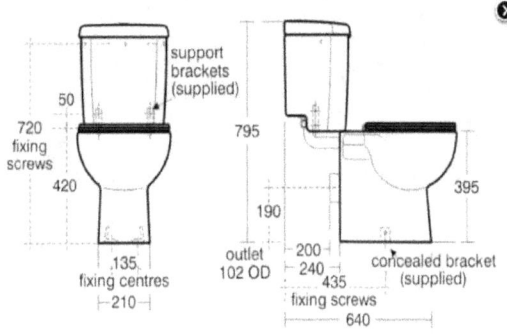

E7172 - Space Close Coupled WC Pan

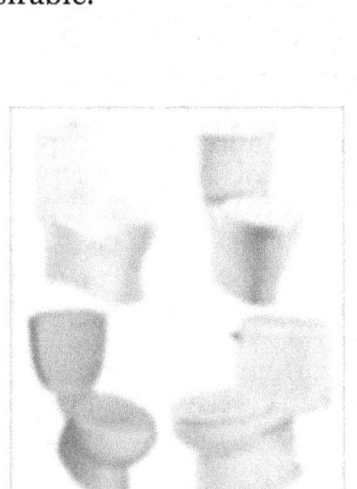

Almost every style and shape of w.c. has a matching bidet such as this wall mounted pair but beware not all and not always readily available - also note the squarish designs of w.c. take a special seat which can be very expensive and some bidets also have a cover available. Rising spray bidets are virtually unavailable and almost impossible to fit because of the new stringent regulations..

SHOWERBATHS

SIZES

standard size 1700/1500

extra large 1800

standard acrylic

heavy duty like carronite

full overbath enclosures

traditional shower screens

p shape or geometric

In the early days a shower bath was an ordinary bath with a screen or enclosure. These are still available but conventional baths are not generally designed for showering over. where space permits the P shape bath or the new geometric shape shower bath is easily the best choice. Although they are a wider at the showering end than a conventional bath you should be able to find this space even in an conventional British bathroom. They are mostly acrylic & there is a flat non slip area for showing. If you decide to remove your bath and install only a shower you make the house less saleable - a point to remember.

Apart from the fact that all showerbaths are left or right handed and varying sizes there is little else to consider for planning purposes except for the plumbing.

However a little point to note when you are conducting a survey - check out the possibility of a stair wedge.   Quite often, especially in the smaller houses, the bathroom is built over the stair wedge and the bath sloping end is built over the stair wedge so when you take out the bath there is a wedge shape lump at the sloping end. You would find it difficult if not impossible to install a shower bath in this kind of layout - check carefully.

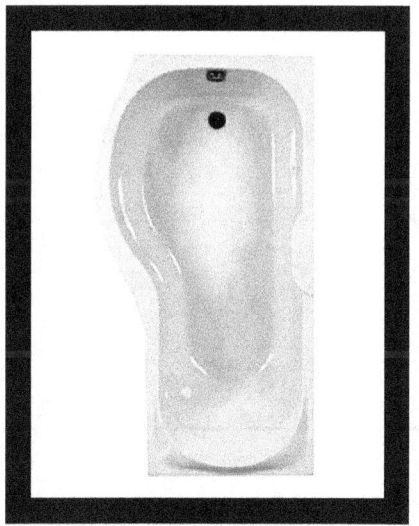

Shower Enclosures

•quadrant - various sizes & handing

•square and rectangular with or without side panels

•trays in different sizes and thicknesses and materials including the latest designer slim line styles

•walk in showers - with proper trays or for use in wet rooms - if the property and installation permits - you need to be very careful with this one

•make sure the quality of the shower suits the showering facility you want - power showers need better enclosures

Gone are the days when a planner would specify a cheap plastic enclosure or one of the old fashioned ideal Standard steel cubicles. Today the choice of showers is a common decision, virtually all executive houses have a separate shower room and many of these 1960's house designs have had their enclosures changed two or three times If they had installed a decent shower and tray in the first instance there would have been no need.

You can also buy steam cabins but this is an entirely different choice and a more niche market so we have left this as a separate subject.

Many buyers now insist on both a shower and a bath in their only bathroom or even in their master bathroom. The medical profession is unanimous in their recommendation of showers. especially where bathrooms are shared by a number of people. Clearly no one wants to bathe in their own or anyone else's filth. Showers have been the biggest growth area in the bathroom market for many. It is probably the most important topic in the majority of bathrooms so study the options carefully.

Your first decision is whether or not to use a shower tray and which style and type to select.

Wet rooms have become a fad but the reality is they are not a great choice for British bathrooms. You will see many successful wet rooms on the continent or in hotels and they are built usually on concrete floors. In the UK with the wooden fabrication of the building, if there is a flaw in the 'tanking' of the wet room, water will inevitably seep out and over a period of years damage the structure of the building. Could be a very expensive error. Use only a very experienced installer or don't do it. Shower trays are now available in 25mm height - you could even flush this with the rest of the floor to achieve a perfect wet room look without the hassle.

When it comes to the choice of shower tray material we have a problem in the UK whereby stone resin trays have been given an undeserved reputation. In fact stone resin trays are very solid but have only a gel coat surface which is frankly, rubbish. What is the most efficient tray is an acrylic tray with it's wonderful durable surface but with a resin backing. Usually found in slimline trays no more than about 50mm thick these are installer friendly and guaranteed for some considerable time, usually a minimum of 10 years.   Choose wisely but do not choose an old fashioned fibreglass tray - these are bigger rubbish than stone resin.

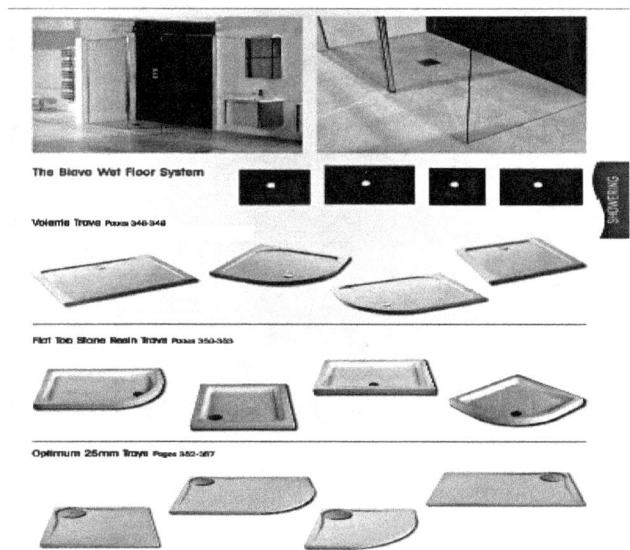

Furniture

Furniture has been a feature of British bathrooms for many years.

•Furniture today tends to be concentrated on modular units rather than fitted bathrooms. There are many of these on the market mostly in high gloss white and, generally speaking ,of European manufacture (Italy and Spain Predominantly) but the Chinese are beginning to offer more in this market sector.

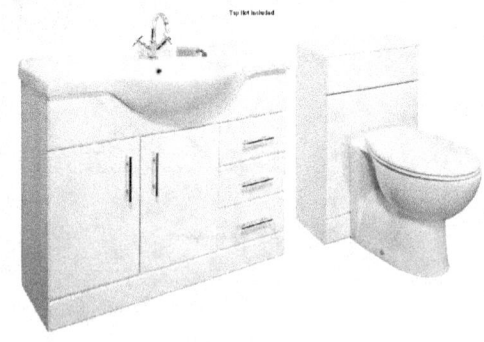

Shower Fittings

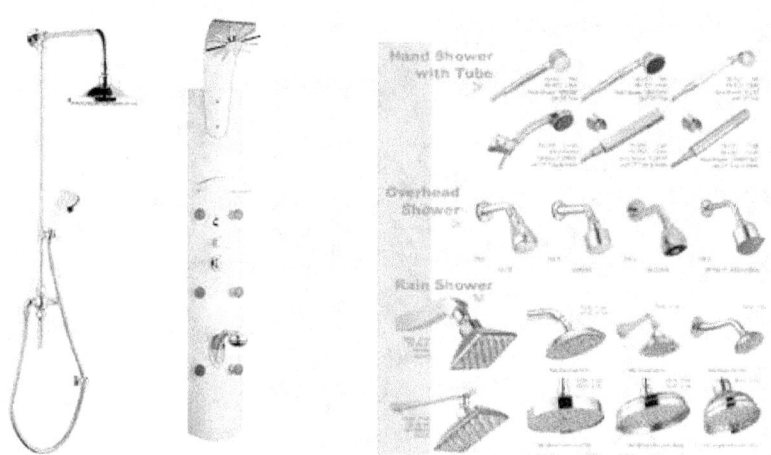

Check the flow rate and match the customer's boiler performance

1.shower tower

2.exposed single lever

3.concealed single lever

4.exposed thermostat

5.concealed thermostat

6.body jets

7.fixed head and slider combi

8.integral pump

9.separate pump

10.eco heads?

Towel Rails and Rads

•for simplicity choose electric

•watch for direct and indirect use

•is it made from mild steel

•is it made from brass

•is it made from copper

•non corrosive is best

•is it meant to heat the room

what is the heat output

Whirlpools and Spa

What is a spa bath, a whirlpool bath, a Jacuzzi bath an airspa bath an airbath . They recirculate air or water AND MUST ALL BE CLEANED -REGULARLY

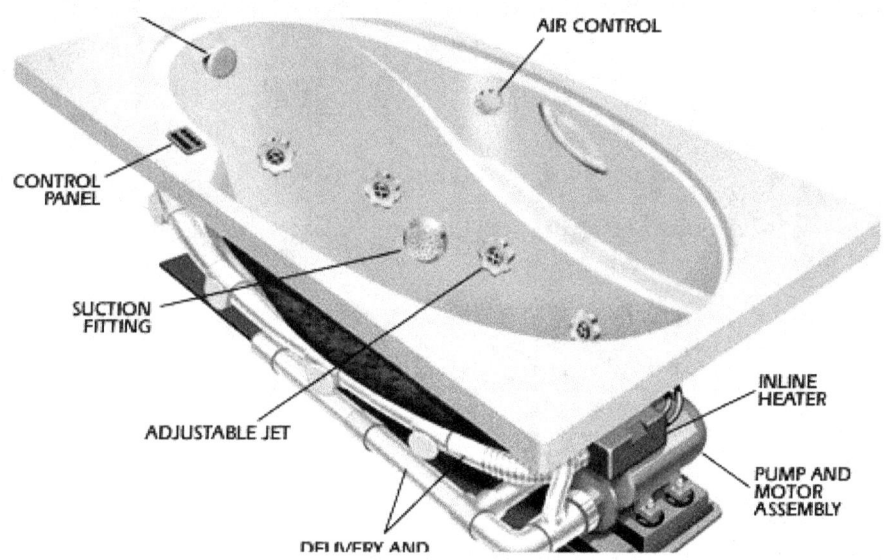

AIR CONTROL

CONTROL PANEL

SUCTION FITTING

ADJUSTABLE JET

DELIVERY AND

INLINE HEATER

PUMP AND MOTOR ASSEMBLY

WHIRLPOOL FEATURES

Standard jets

jacuzzi style jets

micro jets

standard aspiration

turbo - blown aspiration

pneumatic controls

electronic controls

Referring back to our critique of the plan with 2 baths - the reason is the spa bath is used only by adults and because of the build up of human tissue in the pipework it is best to keep kids away.

52

Macerators and Softeners

Because of the drinking water problems softeners are not popular in U.K. but if you choose the right one they can be enormous benefit to the skin. Drink bottled water always.

Macerators can be a life saver to provide a full bathroom facility virtually anywhere in the house and even in a basement. The macerators have a set ability to pump along or pump up or a combination of both. Some are made just for the wc. and others can accept other wastes such as from a basin or shower. MAKE SURE YOU CHOOSE THE CORRECT VERSION - the cost varies

Accessories Mirrors and Lighting

CAN BE HIGH VALUE

These are the little touches that finish your plan and design. It is quite incredible how much they can cost so offer the package as add-ons so the customer can choose according to their budget. Don't overdo it but ensure there is a comprehensive offer within your planning budget.

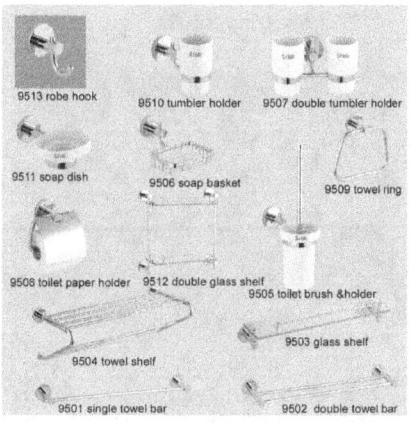

9513 robe hook   9510 tumbler holder   9507 double tumbler holder

9511 soap dish   9506 soap basket   9509 towel ring

9508 toilet paper holder   9512 double glass shelf   9505 toilet brush &holder

9504 towel shelf   9503 glass shelf

9501 single towel bar   9502 double towel bar

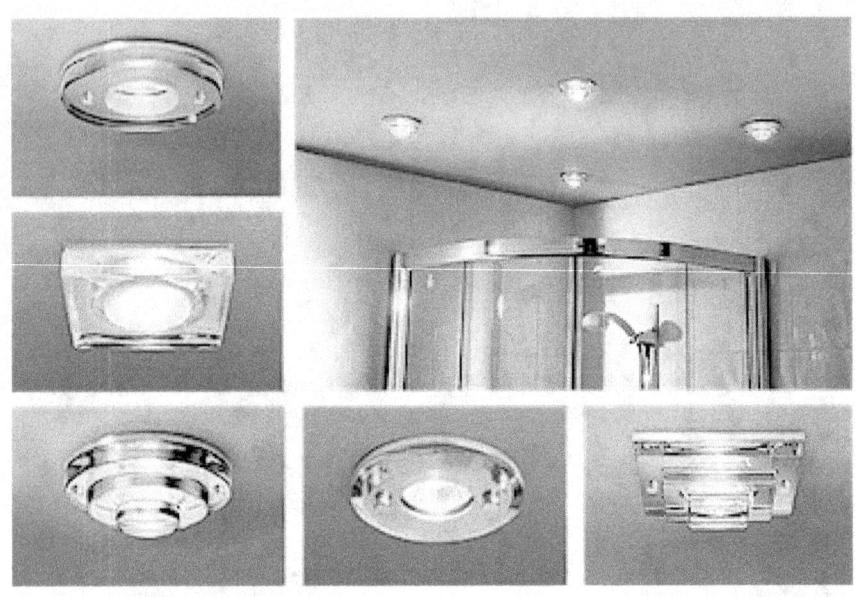

9
Cloakrooms

Remember: cloaks are available in all styles just like the main bathroom.

It is rare to be asked to design a cloakroom but as part of a house remodelling it is a distinct possibility. You may also be asked to design a new cloakroom including the plumbing. You can install a cloakroom anywhere in the property but often only using a macerator. As a cloakroom is mostly for guests it will often be in a less sensitive part of the building where noise is not a bit problem.

10
PRODUCT SUMMARY

comprehensive list of the major bathroom fitments with sized

Basins — measurements in metres
- Medium 0.58 x 0.47
- Semi-Recessed 0.70 x 0.47
- Wing 0.74 x 0.47
- Cloakroom Semi-Recessed 0.50 x 0.38
- Corner 0.64 x 0.49
- Baby 0.47 x 0.30
- Inset / Vessel 0.80 x 0.50
- Block 1.00 x 0.47

Toilets — measurements in metres
- Standard inc portrait Cistern 0.40 x 0.71
- Standard inc Landscape Cistern 0.51 x 0.71
- Corner 0.38 x 0.76
- Back-to-wall & WC unit 0.5 x 0.77

Baths — measurements in metres
- Straight 1.52 x 0.75
- Straight 1.70 x 0.70
- Straight 1.70 x 0.75
- Double Ended 1.70 x 0.75
- Double Ended 1.80 x 0.80
- Freestanding 1.54 x 0.77
- Freestanding 1.70 x 0.77
- Freestanding 1.80 x 0.80
- Showerbath 1.70 x 0.90
- Offset Corner 1.53 x 1.00
- Corner 1.30 x 1.30

Showers — measurements in metres
- Square 0.76 x 0.76
- Square 0.80 x 0.80
- Square 0.90 x 0.90
- Extended 1.20 x 0.76
- Quadrangle 0.90 x 0.90
- Offset Quadrangle 0.90 x 1.20
- Walk-In 1.70 x 0.90

Furniture — measurements in metres
- Base Unit 0.76 x 0.27
- Mirror 1.20 x 0.20
- Mirror 0.70 x 0.20
- Dress Mirror 0.40 x 0.20
- Wall Cabinet 0.40 x 0.27
- Wall Cabinet 0.70 x 0.27
- Wing Shelves 0.25 x 0.25

Bidets — measurements in metres
- Bidet 0.56 x 0.37

SERVICES

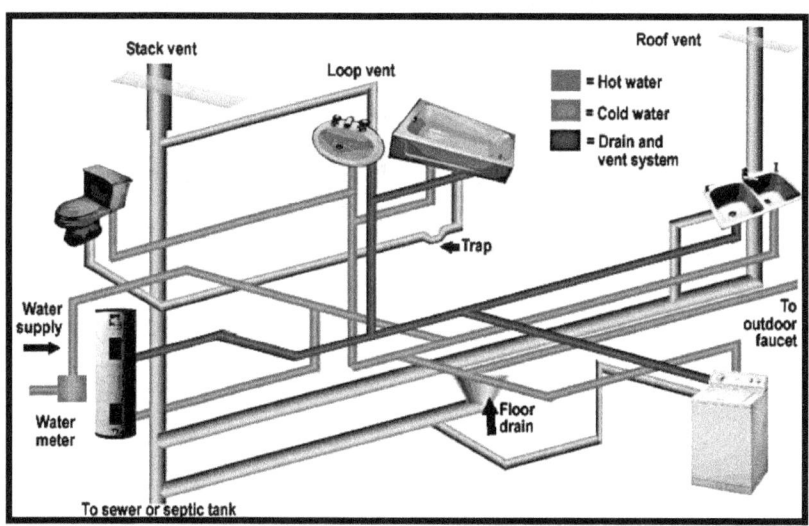

This has long been a problem area. Most delegates don't want to know but to be an efficient designer you have to know at least the basics. I would urge you to at least get to grips with the essentials of DIY services. Clearly the major consideration is the plumbing. Always play safe especially when first starting to plan. Only make major changes when you have the confidence that the plumbing will work.

ELECTRICS

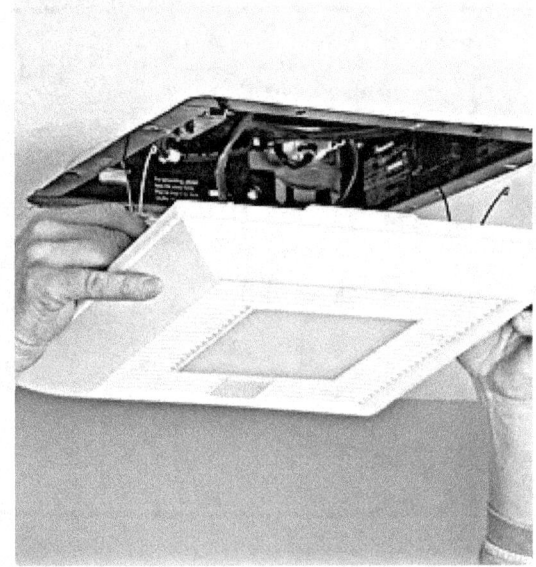

•how extensive is the lighting plan
•any special circuits required such as electric shower
•is there a whirlpool bath with an in line heater
•are additional electrics required
•is there an existing RCD
•will any RCD OR ELCB's interfere with the current or new installation

Electrics are critical in a bathroom. You should by now have covered the section on bathroom zones for electrics and i rating of lighting in the zones within a bathroom. clearly you will also have other electrics in the bathroom such as a whirlpool or other spa bath which requires special consideration. For example a novice electrciain as most plumbers are will probably want to install an ELCB for the whirlpool bath and yet if you already have one on the existing system another

one could become a problem rather than a benefit. also remember that some bathrooms may have high unit items such as a Steam Generator or an Electric Shower. These items could take 30 amps or more. In fact some steam generators need 3 phase which the average household would not have and could not economically install.

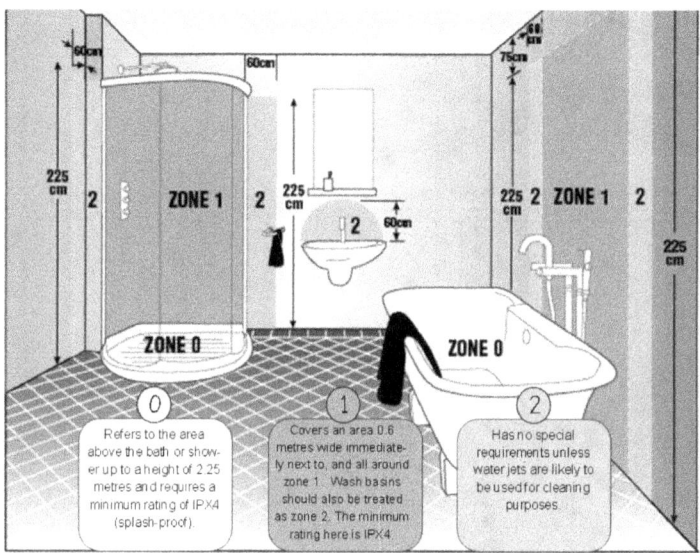

Zone 0 - the interior of the bath or shower that can hold water. Requires electrical products to be low voltage (max 12V) and rated IPX7.

Zone 1 - the area directly above zone 0, limited to a height of 2.25m above the bath or shower. Requires electrical products to have an IPX4 or better. Products should use safety extra low voltage (SELV) with the transformer located in zone 3 or beyond.

Zone 2 - the area beyond zones 0 and 1, stretching 0.6m horizontally and up to 2.25m vertically. Also includes the recessed area of a window with a sill next to the bath. Requires electrical products to have an IPX4 or better. SELV with the transformer located in zone 3 or beyond.

Zone 3 - the area beyond zone 2, stretching 2.4m horizontally and up to 2.25m vertically. There is not a specified IP number for this zone, although some products are marked as not for bathroom use. SELV or shaver units are permitted, all other portable electrical equipment is not.

PLUMBING

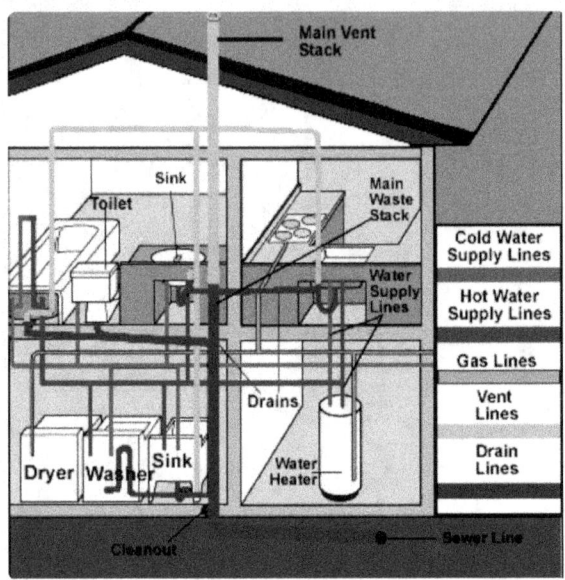

Remember a plumber isn't necessarily a bathroom installer - check him out first - ask around

if you think the job is taking too long it may be worthwhile double checking his credentials

the sign of an amateur plumber is evident when you have to take out an old fashioned cast iron bath. the amateur will try to carry it downstairs - by himself. The professional will bring his sledge hammer and smash it into small pieces.

normal wastes require a 1:20 drop

w.c. waste requires a 1:40 drop

shower wastes require a 1:12 drop for first metre

IF YOU DO NOT PLAN TO INCLUDE THESE DROPS THE WASTE WILL BLOCK.

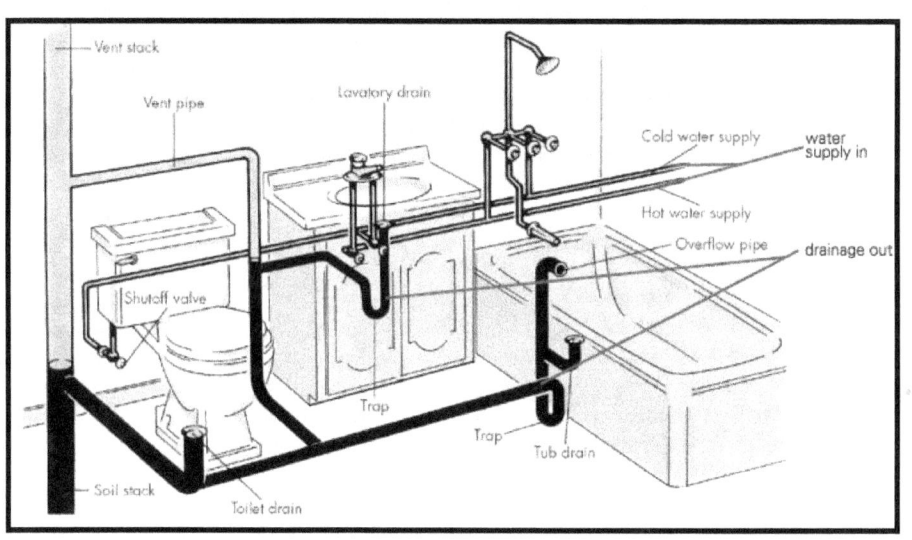

Vent stack

Vent pipe

Lavatory drain

Cold water supply

water supply in

Hot water supply

Overflow pipe

drainage out

Shutoff valve

Trap

Trap

Tub drain

Soil stack

Toilet drain

IMPORTANT POINTS

The average DIYer is competent for simple jobs but when you
encounter the new speedfit plumbing it is easy to get caught lacking
and when it comes to the large soil pipe for the w.c., Bad News -
leave it to the professionals and save yourself a lot of grief. It isn't
cheap but if you get stuck it will cost even more to rectify. And you
probably don't have the best tools such as pipe bending equipment
which can save quite a bit on fittings. Your plumber will have these

Ventilation

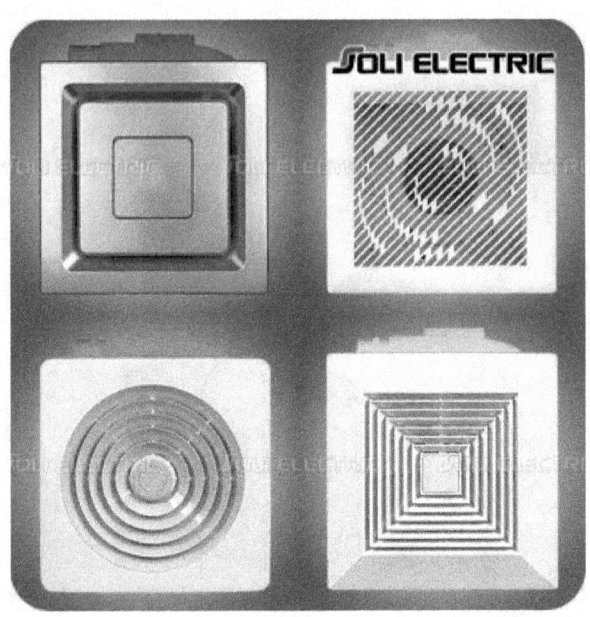

WHY VENTILATE?

* if you have no windows it is the law
* keeps smells at bay
* even if you have a window do you want it open in the winter?
* steam showers must be ventilated
* helps control mold
* keeps bathroom decor fresh and clean and slows deterioration

It has always surprised me that so many people build a lovely new bathroom costing £1000's and don't protect their investment by ventilating the room. Bathrooms are damp anyway and showers are damper still. Control this with a proper adequate sized fan. A variable control with a humidistat would be the best choice but any fan is better than nothing. Best to have one that is controllable rather than just comes on with the light. Often people forget to turn these things off and burn out the motor. Also purchasing a quality product means longer lasting and lower noise levels. Choose and buy wisely. You will find most fans clearly marked with their capability.

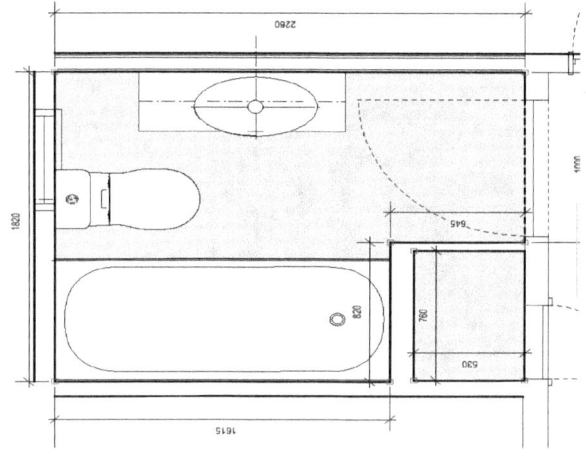

all measurements are mm unless otherwise stated

Having studied this guide we recommend that you attempt a number of exercises. this is the first. You can request further by going to our website at www.kbb2000.com

The Exercise

Study the plan above and draw the room but we are going to incorporate the airing cupboard into the main bathroom.

This gives us plenty of space to incorporate a nice size shower.

Other than that the spec will be the same but it is your choice of bath, basin, w.c. and the size and style of the shower.

The buyer does not need a spa and will be using the bath mainly for their two small children. This is the main bathroom in the house. There is no en suite.

The customer would like a cloakroom fitted downstairs and would welcome any suggestions as to how they would find the space. There is a cupboard under the stairs but it isn't that large but the access to the cupboard is at the end of the hall.

Well I hope you have enjoyed this Mini Guide experience and perhaps you will join us again in another of these Guides. Please remember that the portrait guides are simpler and therefore cheaper than the landscape guides and the planning guides will vary because of the graphic content but the aim is always to produce an inexpensive and convenient guide.

Titles in the Mini Guide 2016 series

KITCHEN PLANNING ESSENTIALS	I POINT PERSPECTIVE & VANISHING POINT
KITCHEN PLANNING APPLIANCES ESSENTIALS	2 POINT PERSPECTIVE & VANISHING POINT
KITCHEN DESIGN	BIRDS EYE PERSPECTIVE
BATHROOM PLANNING	BEDROOM PRESENTATION
BATHROOM DESIGN	BATHROOM PRESENTATION

If you do not see the title you want please enquire via our website kbb2000.com

SURVEYING TECHNIQUES

EXTERIOR PRESENTATIONS

GRANNY FLATS

CLOAK ROOMS DRESSING ROOMS CLOSETS

KITCHEN WORKING TRIANGLE 2016

DOUBLE WORKING TRIANGLE

CREATIVE INTERIOR DESIGN USING A COMPUTER

CAD VS BRAIN